SCHOLASTIC

10 MIN SATs TESTS MATHS

CW00502297

**AGES 8–9
YEAR 4**

KS2

Scholastic Education, an imprint of Scholastic Ltd

Book End, Range Road, Witney, Oxfordshire, OX29 0YD

Registered office: Westfield Road, Southam, Warwickshire CV47 0RA

www.scholastic.co.uk

© 2018, Scholastic Ltd

1 2 3 4 5 6 7 8 9   8 9 0 1 2 3 4 5 6 7

British Library Cataloguing-in-Publication Data

A catalogue record for this book is available from the British Library.

ISBN 978-1407-17525-6

Printed by Bell and Bain Ltd, Glasgow

Author
Paul Hollin

Editorial team
Rachel Morgan, Audrey Stokes, Kate Baxter, Julia Roberts

Series Design
Scholastic Design Team: Nicolle Thomas and Neil Salt

Design
Scholastic Design Team: Alice Duggan

Cover Design
Scholastic Design Team: Nicolle Thomas and Neil Salt

Cover Illustration
Adam Linley @ Beehive Illustration
Visual Generation @ Shutterstock

Illustrations
Technical Artwork: Dave Morris
Figures: Carys Evans
Banknotes: © Bank of England [2015]

Contents

How to use this book

This book contains four different sets of maths tests for Year 4, each containing SATs-style questions. Each set comprises one arithmetic test followed by two reasoning tests. As a whole, the complete set of tests provides full coverage of the test framework for this age group, across the two strands of the maths curriculum: Number; and Measurement, geometry and statistics.

Some questions require a selected response, for example where children choose the correct answer from several options. Other questions require a constructed response, where children work out and write down their own answer.

A mark scheme, skills check and progress chart are also included towards the end of this book.

Completing the tests

- It is intended that children will take approximately ten minutes to complete each individual test; or approximately 30 minutes to complete each set of three tests.

- After your child has completed each set, mark the tests and together identify and practise any areas where your child is less confident. Ask them to complete the next set at a later date, when you feel they have had enough time to practise and improve.

10 MINS

Marks

1. $5 \times 9 =$

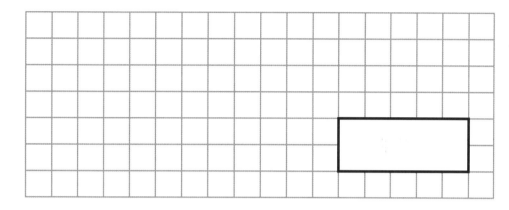

1

2. $25 + 25 + 25 =$

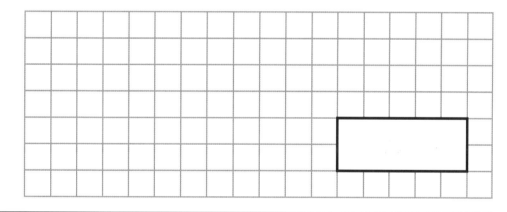

1

3. $21 + 17 =$

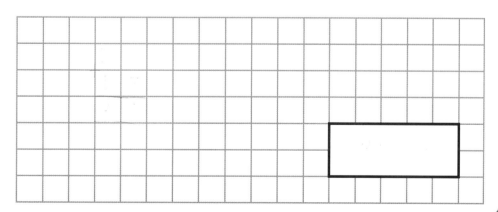

1

5

10 MINS

Marks

4. $39 \div 13 =$

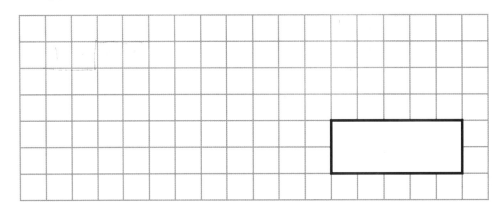

1

5. $\dfrac{3}{5} - \dfrac{1}{5} =$

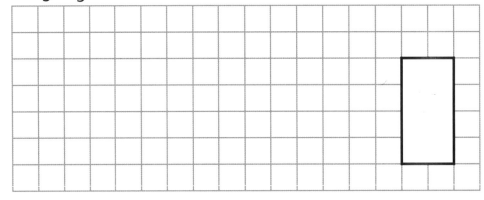

1

6. $36 \div 10 =$

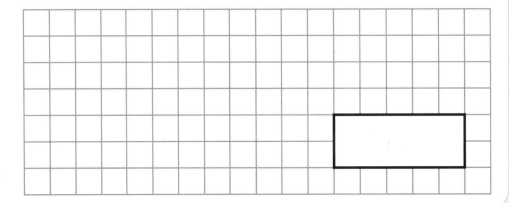

1

10 MINS

Marks

7.   3652 − 2314 =

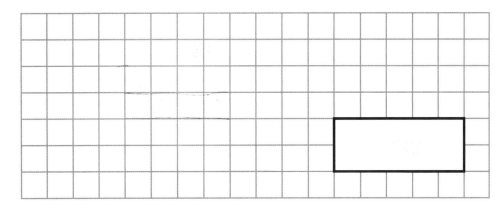

1

8. $\frac{1}{3}$ of 42 =

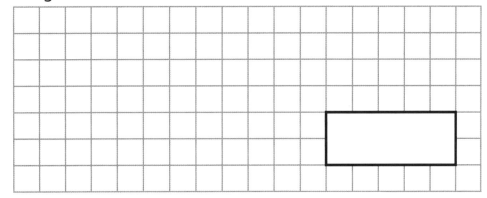

1

9.   3 × 4 × 7 =

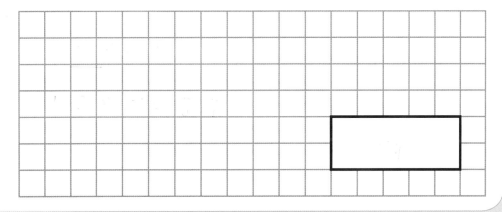

1

10 MINS

10.

Marks

Show your method

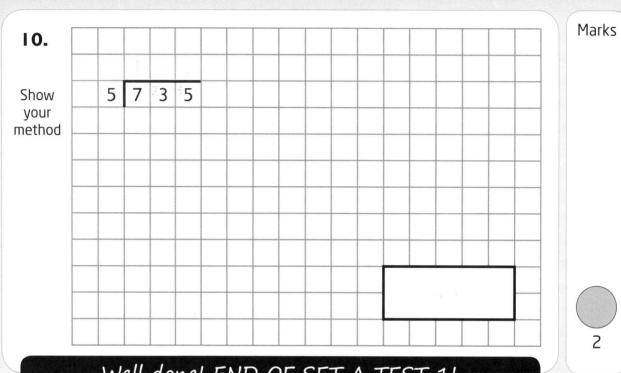

5 | 7 3 5

2

Well done! END OF SET A TEST 1!

1. A square is divided into identical shapes by joining the opposite vertices.

Marks

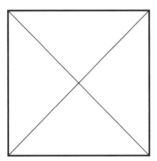

Name of shape: Square.

Contains: 4 right-angled triangles.

Join opposite vertices to divide this regular polygon in the same way, and then fill in the blanks below.

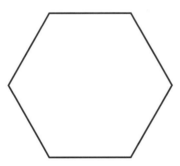

Name of shape: _____

Contains: _____

2

Marks

2. Draw lines to match each Roman numeral to the correct number.

 IX   9

 XC   19

 XIX   90

1

---

3. Kevin's mum says he can have $\frac{1}{4}$ of a bag of popcorn, or 0.3 of the whole bag.

Which do you think Kevin should choose? Explain your answer.

_____

_____

_____

1

10 MINS

Marks

4. This table shows the number of visitors to a museum over three days.

Day	Visitor numbers
Monday	297
Tuesday	255
Wednesday	214

Calculate the total number of visitors rounded to the nearest 10.

Show your method

visitors

2

5. Write the missing digits to complete this addition.

$$
\begin{array}{r}
1\ 6\ \square\ 7 \\
+\ \ 2\ \square\ 3\ 4 \\
\hline
4\ 3\ 9\ 1 \\
\hline
\end{array}
$$

1

10 MINS

6. Leanne went to town to meet her friends. This is how long her journey took.

Marks

Walk to the bus stop: 5 minutes

Wait at the bus stop: 7 minutes

Bus journey to town: 14 minutes

Walk from the bus stop to meet friends: 3 minutes

a. Leanne left the house at 13:50. What time did she meet her friends?

1

b. On her journey to meet her friends, Leanne waited at the bus stop for 420 seconds.

She was on the bus for 840 seconds.

For how many seconds did she walk altogether at the start and end of her journey?

seconds

1

Well done! END OF SET A TEST 2!

Marks

1. Arrange these decimals in order, from smallest to largest.

0.45　　0.34　　0.54　　0.43　　0.53　　0.35

smallest　　　　　　　　　　　　　　　　**largest**

1

2.

A plastic bucket weighs 800g.

A farmer puts 3kg of apples into the bucket.

How much do the bucket and apples weigh altogether?

You can give your answer in kilograms or grams.

1

10 MINS

3. Shade each shape to match it to the equivalent fraction.

Marks

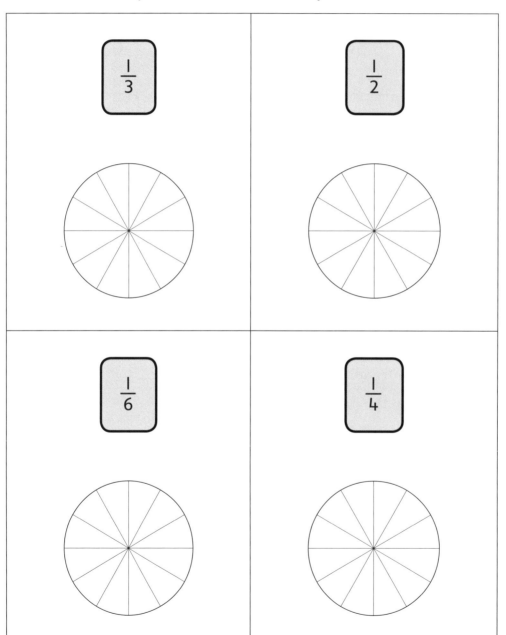

1

10 MINS

4.

Marks

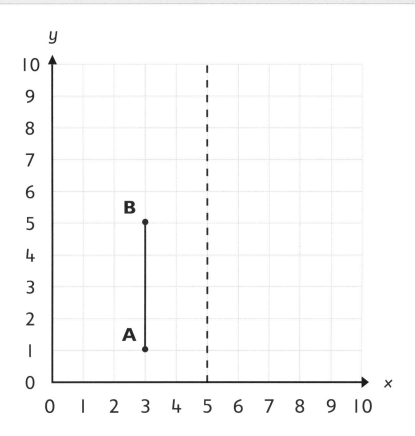

a. Write the coordinates for A and B.

A: (_____ , _____)   **B:** (_____ , _____)

1

b. Draw on the graph the reflection of line AB in the dotted line.

1

KEEP IT GOING!

10 MINS

5. Rachel is given £3.50 pocket money each week.

She saves all of it for 5 weeks and then buys
a new hat for £13.99.

Calculate how much money Rachel will have left.

Marks

Show your method

2

6. Gina's teacher is exactly 1m 80cm tall.

She builds a scale model of her teacher.
The model is 15cm tall.

How many times bigger is her teacher
than the model?

	times bigger

1

Well done! END OF SET A TEST 3!

Set B
Test 1: Arithmetic

10 MINS

Marks

1. $6 + 6 + 6 + 6 =$

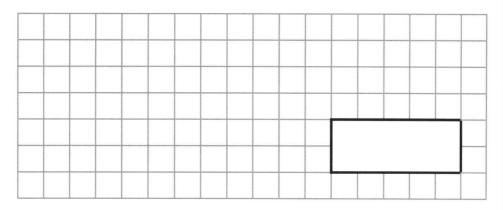

1

2. $30 \div 3 =$

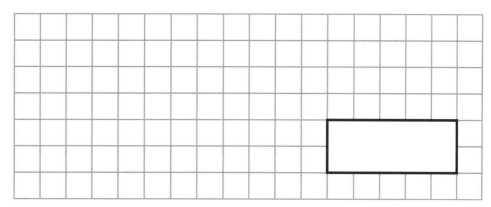

1

3. $6 \times 0 =$

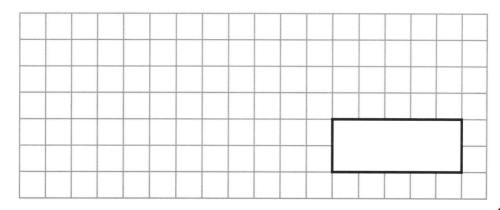

1

Marks

4. $362 + \boxed{} = 880$

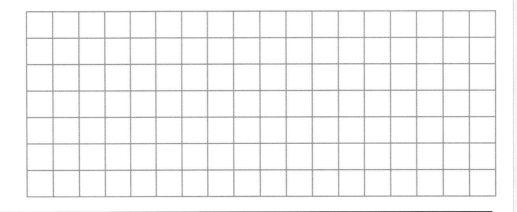

1

5. $1 - \dfrac{2}{7} =$

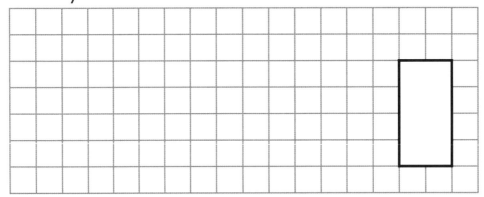

1

KEEP IT GOING!

10 MINS

Marks

6. $7 \times 8 =$

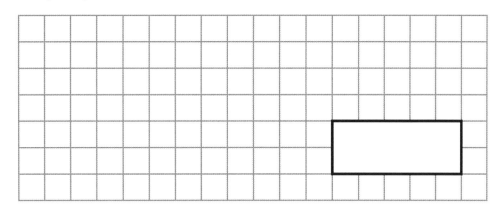

1

7. $14 \div 100 =$

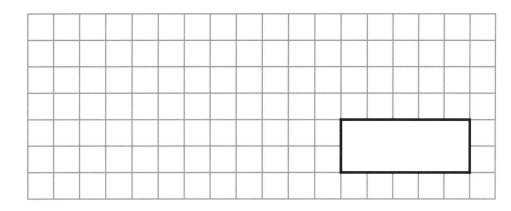

1

8. $6764 + 2451 =$

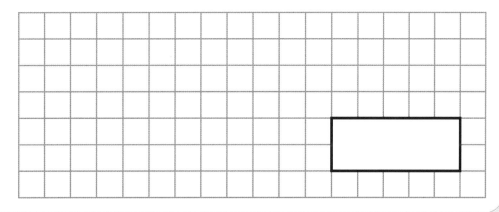

1

Marks

9. $\frac{3}{4}$ of 88 =

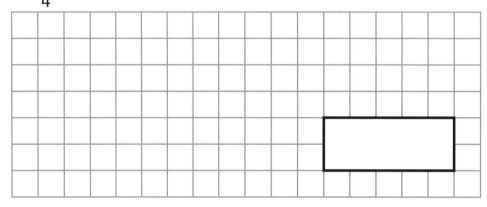

1

10.

Show your method

```
    5 8 1
  ×       6
  ‾‾‾‾‾‾‾‾‾
```

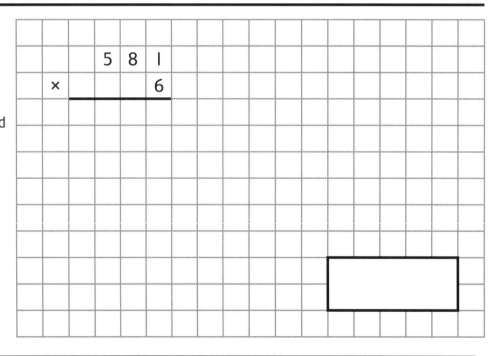

2

Well done! END OF SET B TEST 1!

Set B
Test 2: Reasoning

10 MINS

I. Draw a line of symmetry on this shape.

Marks

1

KEEP IT GOING!

21

10 MINS

Marks

2. Circle the number which is **one thousand less** than this number: eleven thousand, six hundred and eighty-three

     10,000   10,683   11,583   10,583

1

3. A concert is being planned at a theatre for all the schools in a small town.

The table shows the number of children and teachers in each school.

School	Children	Teachers
Aberly	175	6
Bewick	200	7
Conston	230	9

If the theatre has 700 seats and all the children and teachers go to the concert, how many spare seats will there be?

Show your method

spare seats

2

4. Find the area of this shape.

Marks

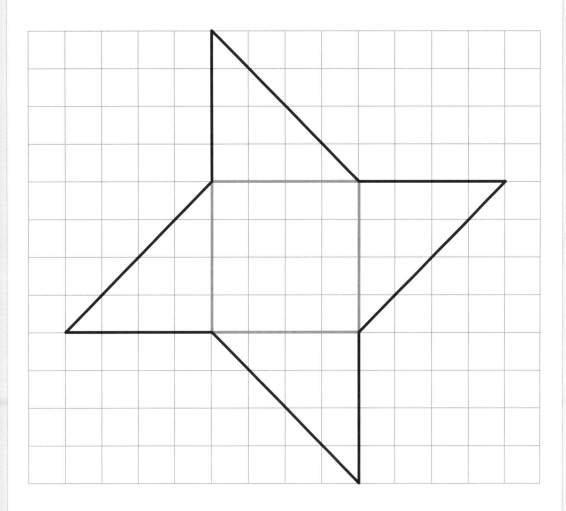

Area = [   ] cm²

1

10 MINS

Marks

5. a. One-sixth of all the sheep in a field are black sheep. If there are four black sheep, how many sheep are there altogether?

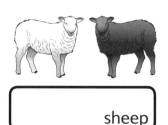

sheep

1

b. The farmer puts another six black sheep in the field. What fraction of all the sheep are now black?

1

6. a. A school running track is 200m. Jenna runs five and a half laps of the track. Circle the two calculations which can be used to show how far Jenna ran.

5.5 × 200

200 + 5.5

200 + 200 + 200 + 200 + 200 + 100

5.5 + 5.5 + 5.5 + 5.5 + 5.5 + 5.5

1

b. How far did Jenna run?

m

1

Well done! END OF SET B TEST 2!

Set B
Test 3: Reasoning

1. Match each decimal to its shaded fraction equivalent. One has been done for you.

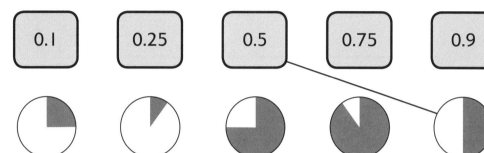

Marks

1

2. Jo does a calculation.

$$45 \times 7 = 315$$

Use an inverse calculation to check if she is right.

Is Jo's calculation correct? Circle the correct answer.

Yes   **No**

1

3. Look at this parallelogram. Its angles have been labelled A, B, C and D.

Marks

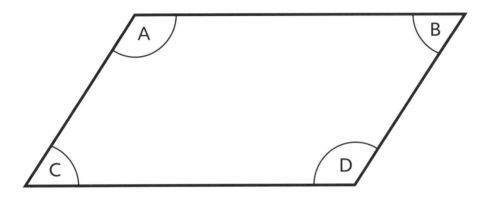

a. Complete these sentences using any of the letters:

Angle _____ is bigger than angle _____.

Angle _____ equals angle _____.

1

b. Now complete these sentences:

Angles _____ and _____ are acute.

Angles _____ and _____ are obtuse.

1

4. a. A camera on a busy motorway shows that 1000 cars go past every twenty minutes.

How many cars will go past in two hours?

Marks

| cars |

1

b. A traffic survey at a local school estimates that 25 cars go past the front gates every five minutes.

How long would it take for 200 cars to go past the school?

Welcome to
Evergreen
Primary School

| minutes |

1

Marks

5. This is a bar chart for pet ownership in a school.

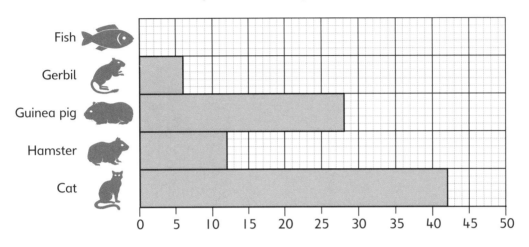

a. 17 children have a fish as a pet. Add this bar to the chart.

1

b. Javid says that **altogether** there are more gerbils, guinea pigs and hamsters than cats. How many more?

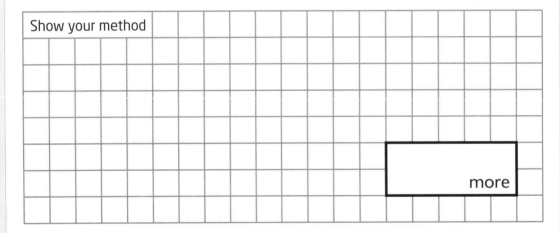

Show your method

more

2

Well done! END OF SET B TEST 3!

Set C

Test 1: Arithmetic

10 MINS

Marks

1. $42 - \boxed{} = 33$

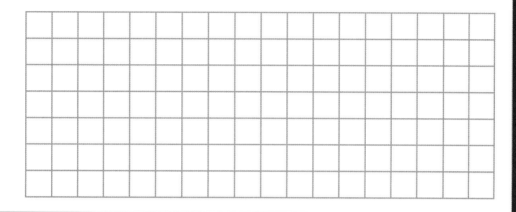

1

2. $\frac{1}{4} + \frac{1}{4} + \frac{1}{4} =$

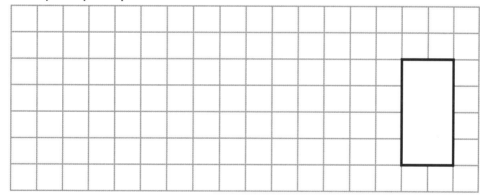

1

KEEP IT GOING!

10 MINS

Marks

3. $5 \times 6 =$

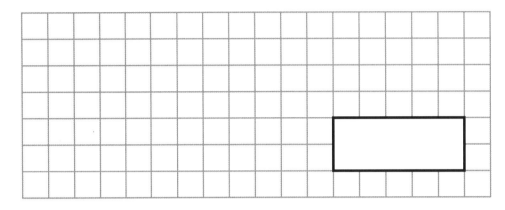

1

4. $7 + 7 + 7 + 7 + 7 =$

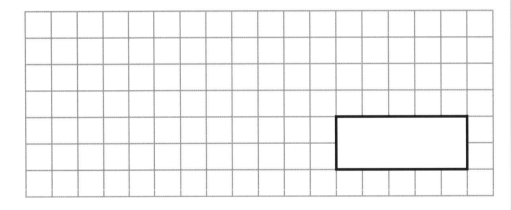

1

5. $910 - 250 =$

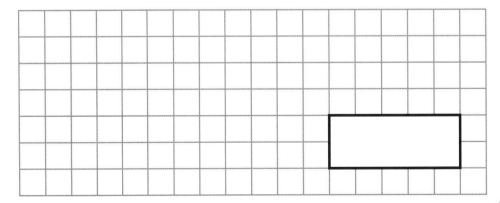

1

6.   38 ÷ 100 =

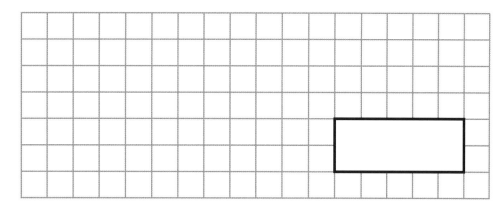

Marks

1

7.   240 ÷ 12 =

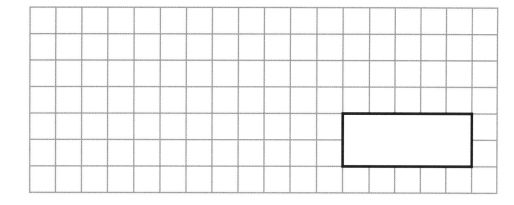

1

8.   9873 + 2142 =

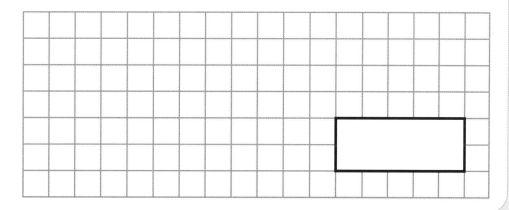

1

Marks

9. $\frac{2}{5}$ of 35 =

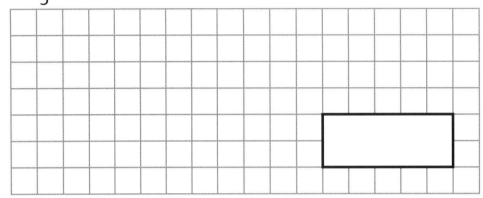

1

10.

Show your method

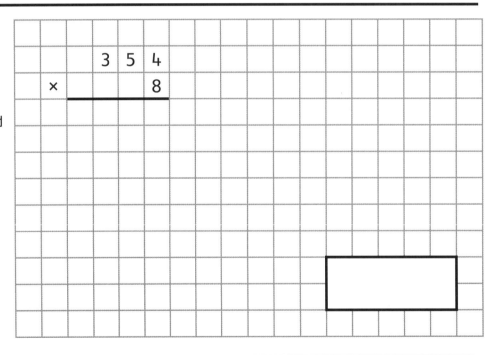

		3	5	4
×				8

2

Well done! END OF SET C TEST 1!

Set C
Test 2: Reasoning

Marks

1. Some fruits have been weighed.

	98g
	1.8kg
	19g
	89g

Write the mass of the fruits in order from lightest to heaviest.

lightest   **heaviest**

1

2. Circle the number that has 7 hundreds.

   73,521   31,725   52,317   17,325   13,275

1

3. Draw the reflection of this shape in the mirror line.
You do not need to shade the reflected shape.

Marks

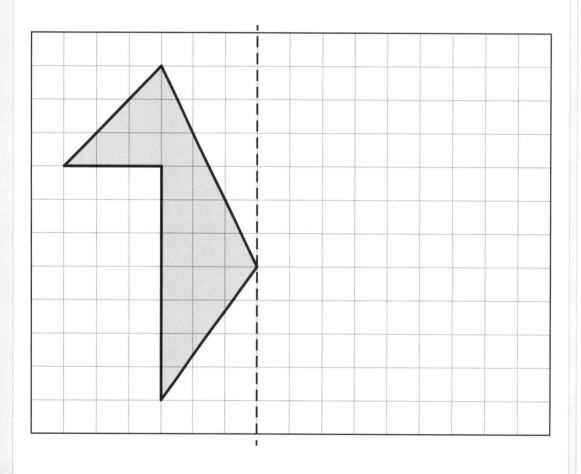

1

Marks

4. Write the missing digits to make this multiplication correct.

$$1\ \boxed{\ }\ 6$$

$$\times \qquad\quad 4$$

$$\overline{5\ \ 4\ \boxed{\ }}$$

1

5. The perimeter of a large square tile is exactly 1m.

Find the perimeter of a rectangle made by joining 4 tiles together.

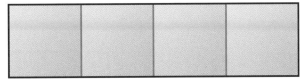

Show your method

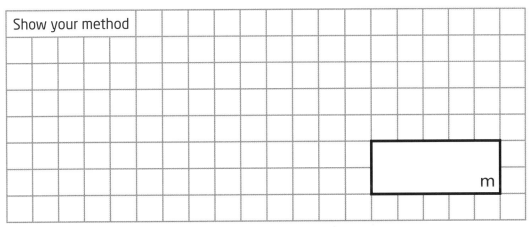

m

2

6. Evan is making cakes.

Recipe

For every 100g of flour, add

2 eggs

80g of sugar

16 raisins

Marks

Evan uses 600g of flour.

a. Calculate how many eggs Evan will need:

eggs

1

b. Calculate how much sugar Evan will need:

g

1

c. Evan already has a packet of 60 raisins. How many more will he need?

raisins

1

Well done! END OF SET C TEST 2!

1. Write each of these numbers in digits, from smallest to largest. One has been done for you.

two thousand, nine hundred and sixty

~~twenty-one~~

eight hundred and forty-five

seven thousand and thirty-seven

21

smallest   **largest**

Marks

1

---

2. This clock shows the time that a TV programme starts in the afternoon.

This digital clock shows the time that the programme ends.

16:10

How many minutes does the programme last?

minutes

1

10
MINS

3. Henaz has started plotting points to make a symmetrical hexagon. Finish plotting the points and draw the hexagon.

Marks

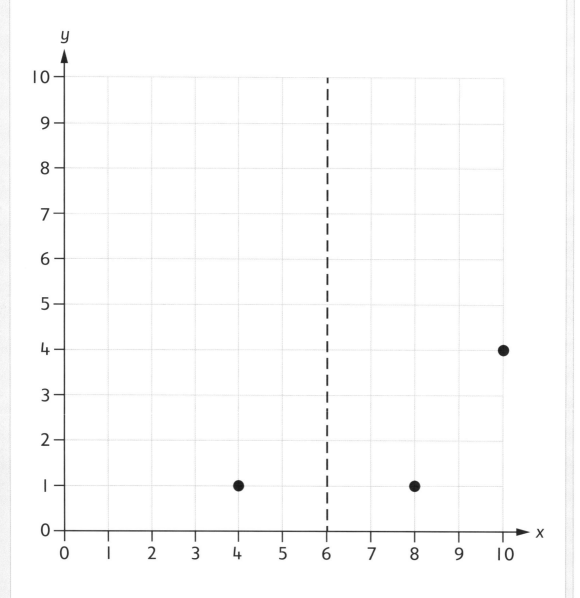

2

4. Nadia wants to buy a maths set. She can buy a complete set, or buy items separately.

Marks

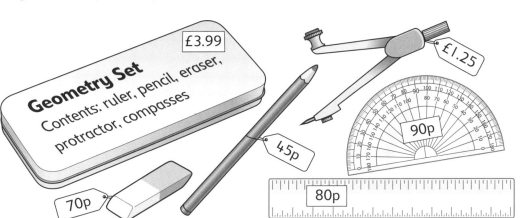

£3.99

Geometry Set
Contents: ruler, pencil, eraser, protractor, compasses

£1.25

90p

45p

70p

80p

How much money can Nadia save if she buys the complete set, rather than the individual items? You can give your answer in pounds or pence.

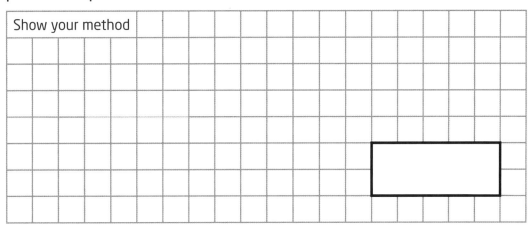

Show your method

2

5. A teacher wants to set some maths problems about the children in her class.

She makes some notes:

> $\frac{1}{4}$ of all the girls have brown eyes.
>
> $\frac{1}{3}$ of the class are boys.
>
> There are 24 children in the class.

Solve this problem.

How many girls in the class **do not** have brown eyes?

Show your method

| | girls |

Marks

2

Well done! END OF SET C TEST 3!

Marks

1. $1 \times 3 \times 4 =$

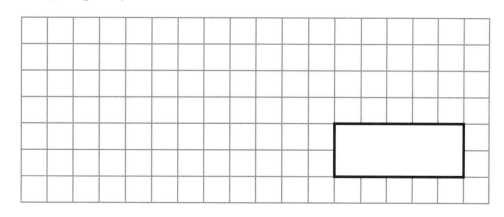

1

2. $0.1 + 0.1 + 0.1 + 0.1 + 0.1 =$

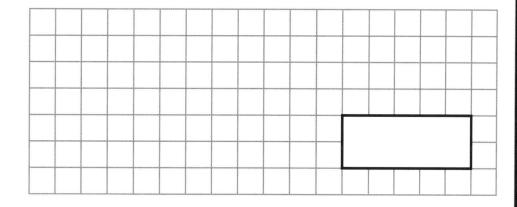

1

3. $73 \div 10 =$

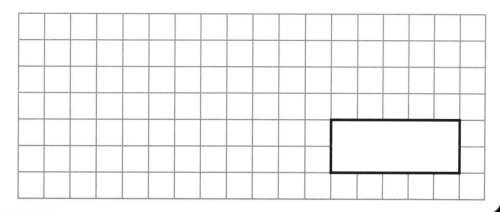

1

10 MINS

Marks

4. $\frac{1}{4}$ of 20 =

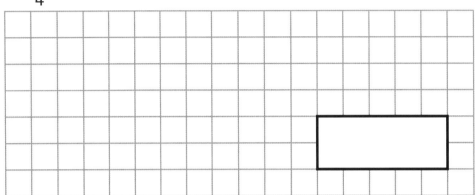

1

5. 56 ÷ ☐ = 8

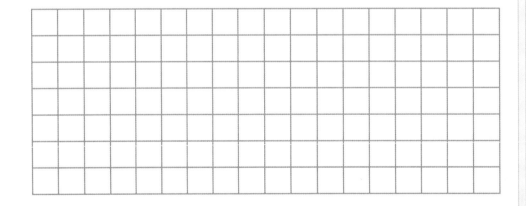

1

KEEP IT GOING!

10 MINS

Marks

6.   11 × 11 =

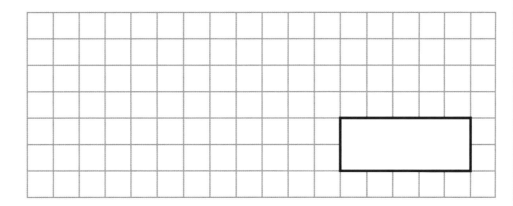

1

7.   458 + 527 =

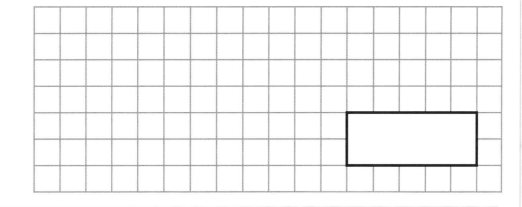

1

8.   6479 − 2514 =

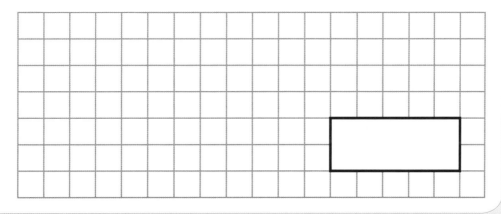

1

10
MINS

Marks

9. $2 - \dfrac{3}{4} =$

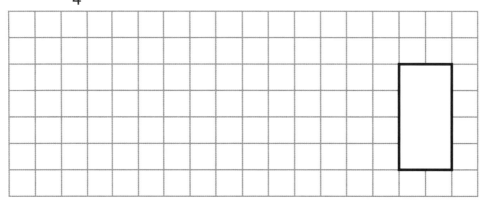

1

10.

Show your method

$7 | 8 \ 8 \ 9$

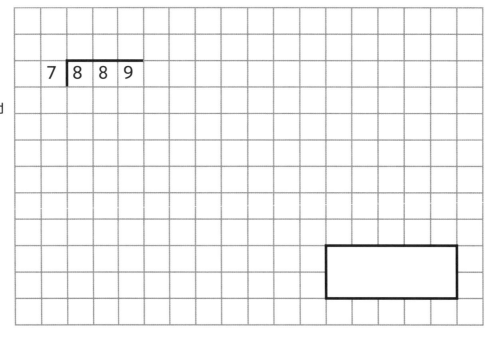

2

Well done! END OF SET D TEST 1!

1. Write the missing digits to make this subtraction correct.

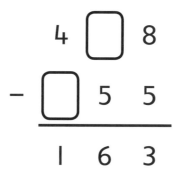

$$
\begin{array}{ccc}
4 & \square & 8 \\
- \ \square & 5 & 5 \\
\hline
1 & 6 & 3 \\
\hline
\end{array}
$$

Marks

1

2. Kerry has more money than Hamza. How much more does she have?

Hamza

Kerry

1

10 MINS

Marks

3. Write the value of each digit in this number. One has been done for you.

6274

6: _____

2: _____

7: _____

4: ___4 ones_____

1

4. A bag has 30 marbles in it.

Larry takes $\frac{1}{5}$ of the marbles; Ben takes $\frac{2}{5}$ and Aisha takes $\frac{1}{5}$.

a. What fraction of the marbles do they take altogether?

1

b. How many marbles will be left in the bag?

marbles

1

5.

Marks

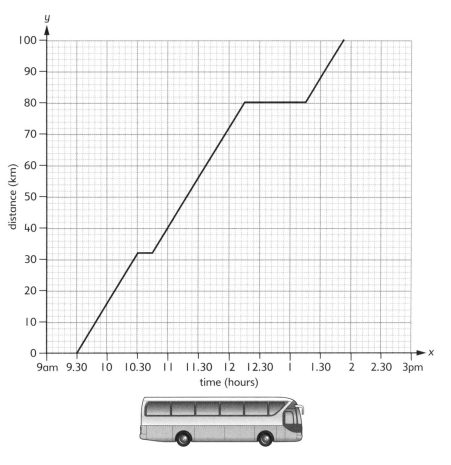

The graph shows a coach journey of exactly 100km.

a. The coach stopped for a short break at 10.30am. How far had it travelled by then?

[ ] km

1

b. The coach then had a longer stop for lunch. What time did the lunch-break end?

[ ]

1

6.

Sally   Wes   Oona   David   Sandeep   Abigail

Marks

Two teams of 3 children play a quick cricket match.

For the first team, Sally scores 47 runs, Wes scores 38 runs, and Oona scores 63 runs.

For the second team, David scores 19 runs and Sandeep scores 85 runs.

How many runs does Abigail have to score **to equal** the first team?

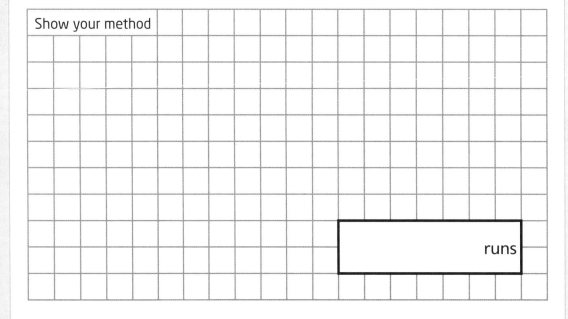

Show your method

runs

2

Well done! END OF SET D TEST 2!

Set D
Test 3: Reasoning

START

1. Ronan says that, rounded to the nearest 10cm, his mum is 170cm tall.

Write the smallest and largest actual height in whole cm that his mum could be.

Smallest height: [ ] cm

Largest height: [ ] cm

Marks

○

1

2. Alice and Sam have 4 pieces of wood.

Each piece is 50cm long and 5cm wide.

Their teacher challenges them to use the pieces of wood to make as large a square as possible.

5cm

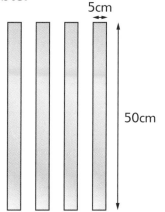
50cm

Find the perimeter of the largest square they can make.

[ ]

○

1

10 MINS

3. Write the missing digits to make this division correct.

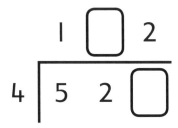

Marks

1

---

4. This 8 × 8 square grid has 64 squares altogether.

It has been shaded in three places.

What fraction of the whole square is each shaded part? Label each of the fractions. Give your answers in the simplest form.

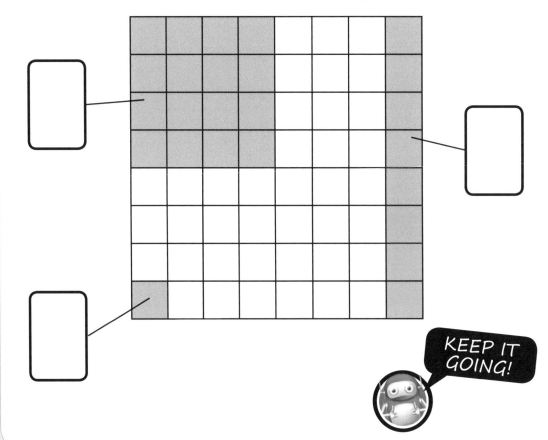

KEEP IT GOING!

1

5.

Marks

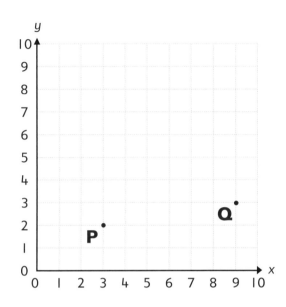

a. Write the translation to move P to Q.

Translation: _____ right and _____ up.

1

b. Translate point Q by moving it 4 left and 5 up. Mark the point on the coordinate grid and label it R.

Write the coordinates of R.

Point R: (_____ , _____)

1

10 MINS

6. Fred is buying his school uniform.

£7.99   £9.99   £8.99

His dad pays with a £20 note and a £10 note.

How much change will he receive?

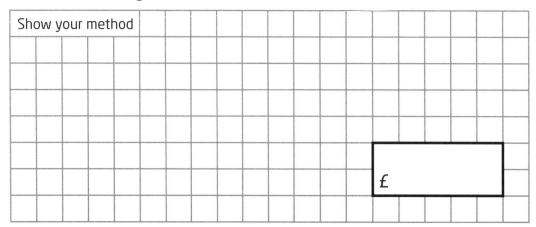

Show your method

£

Marks

2

Well done! END OF SET D TEST 3!

Answers
Maths

Q	Mark scheme for Set A Test 1 – Arithmetic	Marks
1	45	1
2	75	1
3	38	1
4	3	1
5	$\frac{2}{5}$	1
6	3.6	1
7	1338	1
8	14	1
9	84	1
10	147 **Award 1 mark** for a correct method but with one arithmetical error.	2
	Total	11

Q	Mark scheme for Set A Test 2 – Reasoning	Marks
1	Shape: hexagon. Contains: six equilateral triangles. **Award 2 marks** for accurate drawing (all lines accurate within 2mm), correct name of shape and correct name of shapes contained. **Award 1 mark** for accurate drawing (all lines accurate within 2mm) and correct name of shape OR accurate drawing (all lines accurate within 2mm) and correct name of shapes contained.	2
2	IX — 9 XC — 19 XIX — 90	1
3	Answer should show an understanding that $\frac{1}{4}$ (0.25) is less than 0.3. Whether the advice is health or hunger based is not relevant.	1
4	770 people **Award 1 mark** if the initial calculation is correct. **Award 1 mark** for rounding to the nearest 10.	2

Q	Mark scheme for Set A Test 2 – Reasoning	Marks
5	$\begin{array}{r} 1\ 6\ \mathbf{5}\ 7 \\ +\ 2\ \mathbf{7}\ 3\ 4 \\ \hline 4\ 3\ 9\ 1 \end{array}$	I
6	**a.** 14:19 (accept 2.19pm OR 19 minutes past 2) **b.** 480 seconds	I I
	Total	**9**

Q	Mark scheme for Set A Test 3 – Reasoning	Marks
I	0.34 0.35 0.43 0.45 0.53 0.54	I
2	Accept 3.8kg OR 3800g (or grams)	I
3	Note that children may shade any of the segments. To receive one mark they must unambiguously shade the shapes as follows: $\frac{1}{3}$: 4 segments $\frac{1}{2}$: 6 segments $\frac{1}{6}$: 2 segments $\frac{1}{4}$: 3 segments	I
4	**a.** A: (3, 2); B: (3, 6) **b.** Reflected line should be from (7, 2) to (7, 6), drawn accurately to within 2mm of each coordinate. 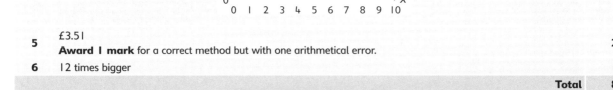	I
5	£3.51 **Award 1 mark** for a correct method but with one arithmetical error.	2
6	12 times bigger	I
	Total	**8**

Q	Mark scheme for Set B Test 1 – Arithmetic	Marks
I	24	I
2	10	I
3	0	I
4	362 + **518** = 880	I
5	$\frac{5}{7}$	I
6	56	I
7	0.14	I
8	9215	I

Q	Mark scheme for Set B Test 1 – Arithmetic	Marks
9	66	1
10	3486 **Award 1 mark** for a correct method but with one arithmetical error.	2
	Total	11

Q	Mark scheme for Set B Test 2 – Reasoning	Marks
1	 Only award mark if line is accurate to within 2mm.	1
2	10,683	1
3	73 spare seats **Award 1 mark** for clear evidence of correct method but with a maximum of one arithmetical error.	2
4	48cm²	1
5	**a.** 24 sheep **b.** $\frac{1}{3}$ (accept $\frac{10}{30}$)	1 1
6	**a.** 5.5 × 200 and 200 + 200 + 200 + 200 + 200 + 100 **b.** 1100m	1 1
	Total	9

Q	Mark scheme for Set B Test 3 – Reasoning	Marks
1		1
2	$\begin{array}{r} 4\ \ 5 \\ 7\,\overline{\smash{\big)}\,3\ \ 1\ \ ^35} \end{array}$ **Award 1 mark** only if correct calculation is clearly shown, and 'yes' has been circled.	1

Q	Mark scheme for Set B Test 3 – Reasoning	Marks
3	In each case, only **award 1 mark** if all answers are correct. **a.** There is more than one possibility for the first two sentences, such as: Angle **D** is bigger than angle **C** OR Angle **D** is bigger than angle **B** OR Angle **A** is bigger than angle **B** OR Angle **A** is bigger than angle **C**. Angle **A** equals angle **D** OR Angle **B** equals angle **C**. **b.** Angles **B** and **C** are acute. Angles **A** and **D** are obtuse.	1 1
4	**a.** 6000 cars **b.** 40 minutes	1 1
5	**a.** 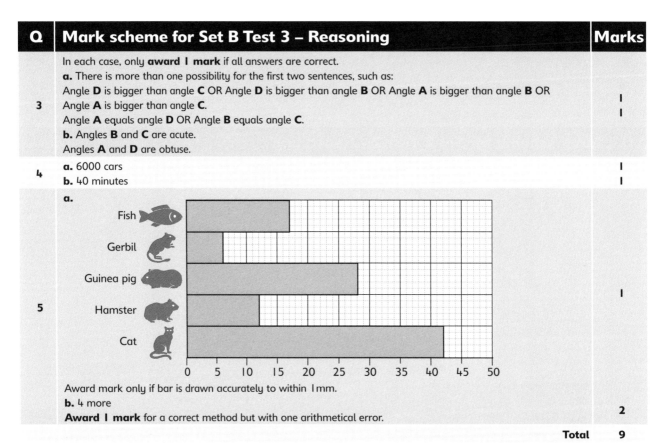 Award mark only if bar is drawn accurately to within 1mm. **b.** 4 more **Award 1 mark** for a correct method but with one arithmetical error.	1 2
	Total	9

Q	Mark scheme for Set C Test 1 – Arithmetic	Marks
1	42 – **9** = 33	1
2	$\frac{3}{4}$	1
3	30	1
4	35	1
5	660	1
6	0.38	1
7	20	1
8	12,015	1
9	14	1
10	2832 **Award 1 mark** for a correct method but with one arithmetical error.	2
	Total	11

Q	Mark scheme for Set C Test 2 – Reasoning	Marks
1	19g, 89g, 98g, 1.8kg	1
2	31,725	1
3	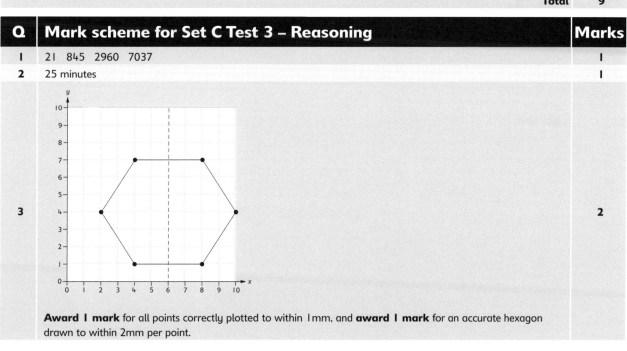 Award mark only if all lines are accurate to within 2mm.	1
4	$\begin{array}{r} 1\ \textbf{3}\ 6 \\ \times\quad\ 4 \\ \hline 5\ 4\ \textbf{4} \end{array}$	1
5	2.5m **Award 1 mark** for a clear demonstration of a correct approach to finding the overall perimeter but with one arithmetical error.	2
6	**a.** 12 eggs	1
	b. 480g	1
	c. 36 raisins	1
	Total	9

Q	Mark scheme for Set C Test 3 – Reasoning	Marks
1	21 845 2960 7037	1
2	25 minutes	1
3		2

Award 1 mark for all points correctly plotted to within 1mm, and **award 1 mark** for an accurate hexagon drawn to within 2mm per point.

Q	Mark scheme for Set C Test 3 – Reasoning	Marks
4	£0.11 OR 11p **Award 1 mark** for a correct approach to solving the answer, but with a maximum of one arithmetical error.	2
5	12 girls do not have brown eyes. **Award 1 mark** for a correct approach to solving the answer, but with a maximum of one arithmetical error.	2
	Total	8

Q	Mark scheme for Set D Test 1 – Arithmetic	Marks
1	12	1
2	0.5	1
3	7.3	1
4	5	1
5	$56 \div 7 = 8$	1
6	121	1
7	985	1
8	3965	1
9	$1\frac{1}{4}$ OR $\frac{5}{4}$	1
10	127 **Award 1 mark** for a correct method but with one arithmetical error.	2
	Total	11

Q	Mark scheme for Set D Test 2 – Reasoning	Marks
1	$$\begin{array}{r} 4\ 1\ 8 \\ -\ 2\ 5\ 5 \\ \hline 1\ 6\ 3 \end{array}$$	1
2	22p	1
3	6: **6 thousands** 2: **2 hundreds** 7: **7 tens** 4: 4 ones Accept singular or plurals (for example six thousand/six thousands)	1
4	a. $\frac{4}{5}$ b. 6 marbles	1 1
5	a. 32km b. 1.15pm (accept 13:15)	1 1
6	44 runs **Award 1 mark** for a correct approach to solving the answer, but with a maximum of one arithmetical error.	2
	Total	9

Q	Mark scheme for Set D Test 3 – Reasoning	Marks
1	Smallest: 165cm Largest: 174cm	1
2	Accept 220cm OR 2.2m OR 2m and 20cm	1
3	$\begin{array}{r} 1\ \ 3\ \ 2 \\ \hline 4\ \big|\ 5\ \ 2\ \ \mathbf{8} \end{array}$	1
4		1
5	**a.** Translation: **6** right and **1** up. **b.** R: (5, 8) – only award mark if point is also marked accurately on the coordinate grid, to within 1mm.	1 1
6	£3.03 **Award 1 mark** for a correct approach to solving the answer, but with a maximum of one arithmetical error.	2
	Total	8

Skills check
Maths

General notes for parents and teachers:

- In the National Curriculum tests at Year 6, approximately 85% of marks are from the Place Value, Addition and Subtraction, Multiplication and Division, Fractions, Ratio and proportion and Algebra content areas.

- Where a statement below indicates that the skill should be completed mentally, rough jottings are acceptable.

Number – number and place value

I can count in multiples of 6, 7, 9, 25 and 1000, for example 0, 25, 50, 75, 100, 125...

I can find 1000 more or less than a given number, for example 1000 less than 6273 is 5273.

I can count backwards through zero to include negative numbers, for example $3 - 5 = -2$.

I can recognise the place value of each digit in a 4-digit number (thousands, hundreds, tens, and ones), for example the 8 in 3805 is worth 800.

I can order and compare numbers beyond 1000, for example $3638 > 2978$

I can identify, represent and estimate numbers using different representations, for example numbers as measures: the ball weighs 1250g.

I can round any number to the nearest 10, 100 or 1000, for example 4592 is 4600 to the nearest hundred.

I can solve number and practical problems that involve all of the above and with increasingly large positive numbers, for example estimate the value of $242 + 479 + 685$ to the nearest ten (1410).

I can read Roman numerals to 100 (I to C) and know that over time, the numeral system changed to include the concept of zero and place value, for example my dad is **54**. His age in Roman numerals is **LIV**.

Number – addition and subtraction

I can add and subtract numbers with up to 4 digits using the formal written methods of columnar addition and subtraction where appropriate, for example

```
    5  2  3  7
+   2  0  8  2
   ‾‾‾‾‾‾‾‾‾‾
    7  3  1  9
   ‾‾‾‾‾‾‾‾‾‾
          ₁
```

I can estimate and use inverse operations to check answers to a calculation, for example 5237 + 2082 is approximately 7000. Also, 7329 – 2082 = 5237 so the above addition must be correct.

I can solve addition and subtraction two-step problems in contexts, deciding which operations and methods to use and why, for example Oona buys a book for £8 and a pen. If she receives £6 change from £20, how much did the pen cost?

Number – multiplication and division

I can recall multiplication and division facts for multiplication tables up to 12 × 12, for example 108 ÷ 12 = 9.

I can use place value, known and derived facts to multiply and divide mentally, including: multiplying by 0 and 1; dividing by 1; multiplying together three numbers, for example 2 × 3 × 4 = 24.

I can recognise and use factor pairs and commutativity in mental calculations, for example 20 = 5 × 4 or 4 × 5.

I can multiply 2-digit and 3-digit numbers by a 1-digit number using formal written layout, for example

$$
\begin{array}{r}
3\ 1\ 4 \\
\times\quad\ \ 3 \\
\hline
9\ 4\ 2 \\
\end{array}
$$

I can solve problems involving multiplying and adding, including using the distributive law to multiply 2-digit numbers by one digit for example $37 \times 2 = 30 \times 2 + 7 \times 2 = 74$ (distributive law), integer scaling problems and harder correspondence problems such as n objects are connected to m objects. Or scaling: if a model is 20 times smaller than a real car, how big will a car be for a 12cm model? (2.4m)

Number – fractions (including decimals)

I can recognise and show, using diagrams, families of common equivalent fractions, for example $\frac{1}{2} = \frac{3}{6}$.

I can count up and down in hundredths; recognise that hundredths arise when dividing an object by one hundred and dividing tenths by ten, for example $5 \div 100 = \frac{5}{100}$.

I can solve problems involving increasingly harder fractions to calculate quantities, and fractions to divide quantities, including non-unit fractions where the answer is a whole number, for example $\frac{2}{3}$ of 12 = 8.

I can add and subtract fractions with the same denominator, for example $\frac{4}{7} - \frac{3}{7} = \frac{1}{7}$.

I can recognise and write decimal equivalents of any number of tenths or hundredths, for example $\frac{3}{10} = 0.3$; $\frac{74}{100} = 0.74$.

I can recognise and write decimal equivalents to $\frac{1}{4}$, $\frac{1}{2}$, $\frac{3}{4}$, for example $\frac{1}{4} = 0.25$.

I can find the effect of dividing a 1- or 2-digit number by 10 and 100, identifying the value of the digits in the answer as ones, tenths and hundredths, for example $145 \div 100 = 1.45$.

I can round decimals with one decimal place to the nearest whole number, for example 2.7 rounds to 3.

I can compare numbers with the same number of decimal places up to two decimal places, for example $0.36 < 0.41$.

I can solve simple measure and money problems involving fractions and decimals to two decimal places, for example I have £12.43 in my pocket, and I buy some food for £3.59. How much money will I still have? (£8.84)

Measurement

I can convert between different units of measure, for example kilometre to metre; hour to minute, for example 3 hours = 180 minutes.

I can measure and calculate the perimeter of a rectilinear figure (including squares) in centimetres and metres, for example a square of side 4.5m has a perimeter of $4 \times 4.5 = 18$m.

I can find the area of rectilinear shapes by counting squares, for example a rectangle has two rows of three 1cm^2 squares. Its area is 6cm^2.

I can estimate, compare and calculate different measures, including money in pounds and pence, for example £2.50 > 245p

I can read, write and convert time between analogue and digital 12- and 24-hour clocks, for example 08:30 = half past eight in the morning, or 8.30am.

I can solve problems involving converting from hours to minutes; minutes to seconds; years to months; weeks to days, for example John goes running for 30 minutes 4 times a week. How many hours does he spend running in a week?

Geometry – properties of shape

I can compare and classify geometric shapes, including quadrilaterals and triangles, based on their properties and sizes, for example explain the difference between a rhombus and a square.

I can identify acute and obtuse angles and compare and order angles up to two right angles by size, for example 89° is an acute angle, and is smaller than 125°, which is an obtuse angle.

I can identify lines of symmetry in 2D shapes presented in different orientations, for example a diamond.

I can complete a simple symmetric figure with respect to a specific line of symmetry, for example complete the other half of this drawing of a butterfly.

Geometry – position and direction

I can describe positions on a 2D grid as coordinates in the first quadrant, for example the point A has coordinates (6, 3).

I can describe movements between positions as translations of a given unit to the left/right and up/down, for example to get from A to B, move 2 left and 4 up.

I can plot specified points and draw sides to complete a given polygon, for example the first three vertices of a square have coordinates (2, 3), (6, 3), (6, 7), so the last vertex must be at (2, 7).

Statistics

I can interpret and present discrete and continuous data using appropriate graphical methods, including bar charts and time graphs, for example use the graph to decide which day of the week had the most rainfall.

I can solve comparison, sum and difference problems using information presented in bar charts, pictograms, tables and other graphs, for example how many more hours of sunshine were there on Wednesday than Monday?

Progress chart

Fill in your score in the table below to see how well you've done.

	Score
Set A Test 1	
Set A Test 2	
Set A Test 3	
Set B Test 1	
Set B Test 2	
Set B Test 3	
Set C Test 1	
Set C Test 2	
Set C Test 3	
Set D Test 1	
Set D Test 2	
Set D Test 3	
TOTAL	

Mark	
0–38	Good try! You need more practice in some topics – ask an adult to help you.
39–79	You're doing really well. Ask for extra help for any topics you found tricky.
80–113	You're a 10-Minute SATs Test maths star – good work!

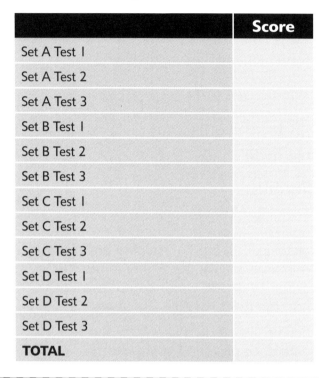

GREAT WORK!

Well done!

You have completed all of the 10-Minute SATs Tests

Name: _____

Date: _____